in' your

Pocket

*To Daisie
With Love and Blessings
Kate West xx*

KATE WEST

ELEMENT

Element
An Imprint of HarperCollins*Publishers*
77–85 Fulham Palace Road
Hammersmith, London W6 8JB

The Element website address is:
www.elementbooks.co.uk

ELEMENT

First published by Element Books 2002

1 3 5 7 9 10 8 6 4 2

A catalogue record of this book
is available from the British Library

ISBN 0 00 714664 7

Printed and bound in Great Britain by
Martins the Printers Limited, Berwick upon Tweed

CONTENTS

INTRODUCTION

Merry Meet and welcome to *Spell in Your Pocket*. Within these pages you can discover how the Magic of Witchcraft can be practised by anyone who wishes to, even in this, our modern, crowded world. Welcome to a new way of thinking where you can take charge of your life and your destiny.

This handy-sized guide (small enough to fit discreetly into your pocket!) is divided into two parts. In Part One you will find a basic introduction to Witchcraft (or 'the Craft', as it is also known), including a self-dedication ritual for becoming a Witch.

Part Two talks about Spellcraft – how magic works, and how to make it work for you. Here you will find information on the tools of magic, and some spells, charms and potions to help you bring natural enhancement to every aspect of your life.

Enjoy this mini-guide to the art and craft of Witchcraft.

Blessed Be.

Kate

PART 1:

ALL ABOUT WITCHCRAFT

CHAPTER ONE

WITCHCRAFT
– THE MYTHS

'Fair is foul and foul is fair …'

Witches are normal everyday people, the kind you pass on the street without giving them a second glance or thought. They are men and women from all age groups, who have all kinds of jobs and normal family lives. They are just like everyone else; in fact they could be just anyone else. But you wouldn't think that if you were to look at the myths that have grown up about them.

The word 'Witch' conjures up many images. A Witch was a woman (for it usually was a woman) who lived on the edge of the village and who would help heal the sick if treated well, but curdle your milk and spoil your crops if you upset her – or even curse your cattle, or your children, so that they would sicken and die. In return for her immortal soul she would have made a pact with the Devil for unnatural powers. And the Devil himself would accompany her in the form of a familiar, who in turn would feed off her flesh. Such Witches were supposed to gather together, flying by broomstick, so that they could join orgies and meet the Devil in person.

A Witch might also be the old hag living alone in a tumbledown cottage in the forest, feared by all. In fairy tales, she would lure innocent children inside to eat them and drink their blood. Or the Witch might be a wicked fairy, not invited to the feast, who would curse the family as a result.

More recently the Witch's image has been influenced by books, music, films and TV. From *Bell, Book and Candle* to *The Craft*, *Bewitched* to *The X-Files* and *Buffy the Vampire Slayer*, Witches are now frequently portrayed as younger, attractive women. They are shown as having control over others. Using ancient powers they perform strange rituals (with lots of modern special effects) and conjure up spirits who do their bidding. They are seen to make people fall in love, to gain revenge on their enemies and even to conjure up uncompleted homework! In fiction they are often linked to Satanists, whose extensive powers enable them to live in improbably wonderful houses. And somehow along the way, Witches have been

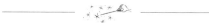

linked to the imagery of Goth and other forms of music, with their vampiric fashions, archaic black clothing, heavy make-up and jewellery.

Other things linked to Witchcraft include broomsticks, cauldrons and black cats, hooked noses, warts, pointed hats and billowing cloaks (black of course). The Full Moon and Halloween are thought to be especially 'Witchy' times.

Now, within these stories and images there are elements of truth, but they are hidden by exaggerations, fabrications and even political intrigue. To understand how these images arose, it is necessary to know a little about the background and history of the Craft.

HISTORY OF THE CRAFT

Before Christianity became established (anything from 1,600 to 800 years ago in various parts of Europe), there were other belief systems. Often called nature religions, these were based around the phases of the Moon, the cycles of the seasons, the land and the animals which lived on it. Different groups held different beliefs and worshipped different Gods and Goddesses, without conflict as far as we know. Roman Gods and Goddesses had shrines or temples alongside those of the native population. At first Christianity was just another belief system and its churches also co-existed peacefully. However, as it became linked with the Crown and the Government it became more powerful and in order to maintain control it sought to eradicate those earlier beliefs.

The Gods of the nature religions now came to be called devils or demons and their followers were accused of laying curses and practising foul Magic which ruined crops, sickened cattle and caused children to fall ill or to die. They were even accused of child murder and sacrifice. Stories were invented or altered to discourage people, especially children, from seeking to learn more. Special agents were appointed to hunt out the 'evil

doers'. Special laws were introduced to cover their 'crimes'. Incentives, in terms of the land and money of those convicted, were provided to encourage people to report those neighbours and fellow villagers who might be involved in such 'demonic' activities.

As a result of the Church's actions many innocent people were arrested, many were tortured and many were executed, some lawfully, others by the mob. Those who did wish to continue to follow the old religions did so secretly. They handed down their knowledge and beliefs by word of mouth, and held their celebrations away from prying eyes. From the outside it appeared that Witchcraft had become a thing of the past, so much so that by the 1950s it was no longer seen as a threat in Britain. The final remnants of the Witchcraft Act, first instituted in 1542, were finally repealed and Witches started, cautiously, to become more open once again.

Some Misconceptions about the Craft

The last 50 years have seen a great improvement in the way that people think about Witches and the Craft and media coverage is more favourable, but there are still many misconceptions and I would like to address a few of them here:

Witches are in league with the Devil
and the same as Satanists.

Witches do not believe in, let alone worship, a devil. They do not believe in an evil being whose purpose is to balance out the good God. Witches believe in personal responsibility – we are each responsible for whatever we do, whether good or bad, and can blame no outside force (or devil) for those actions which we subsequently regret.

WITCHES PRACTISE BLACK MAGIC.

Magic itself is neither good nor bad, white nor black, it is a neutral force in the same way as electricity is. If Magic is used in a positive and beneficial way it is often called 'white'; when used negatively it is often referred to as 'black'. However, most Witches try to adhere to the main 'rule' of the Craft, the Wiccan Rede, which states 'An' it harm none, do what thou will.' Whilst there are undoubtedly a few Witches who do work Magic for selfish reasons or to the detriment of others, the vast majority of Magical workings are for the benefit of others.

WITCHES HAVE A HOOKED NOSE AND WARTS.

As I once said in an interview, 'Well, I wouldn't be much of a Witch if I couldn't get rid of those!' Spreading the idea that Witches are ugly is simply another way of discouraging people from becoming interested in something that is not understood.

WITCHES ARE GLAMOROUS.

This is a more modern misconception. A lot of people believe, without thinking, that Witches all look like Buffy and Sabrina, etc., and that it is the Witchcraft which makes them look good. This is only accurate in that practising the Craft will make you feel better about yourself and encourage you to have respect for your mind, body and spirit. Additionally, because for most of us the imperfections we perceive are false or exaggerated, the self-honesty that the Craft requires will result in a more positive self-image.

YOU CAN TELL A WITCH BY THE WAY THEY LOOK.

When it comes to appearance you cannot tell a Witch by the way they look – Witches are as individual as anyone else. They are not instantly recognizable by their clothes or the way they look. The modern image of the Witch dressed in black with long black hair, pale skin and darkened eyes, hung about with chains of silver, is partly generated by movies and TV, and partly by a fashion trend which some people are enjoying at present. Black clothing, make-up and jewellery are fashion accessories or personal statements about the way you feel and the group you feel comfortable with, not requirements for Witchcraft.

But by far the most insidious myth about the Craft is that Witchcraft makes life easier. Witchcraft does *not* make life easier. As a Witch, you will not have fewer problems, you will probably have more. Witchcraft is about hard work, study and self-discipline.

For anyone who thinks that the Craft will make their life easier I would recommend that they give serious thought to the Wiccan Rede and the Rule of Three, both of which are explained in more detail in the next chapter.

CHAPTER TWO

WITCHCRAFT
IN REALITY

'A Witch is healer, teacher and parent ...'

Having looked at the misconceptions people have about Witches and Witchcraft, let us look at what Witches do believe in and practise.

One of the best definitions I have heard for a Witch is 'healer, teacher and parent'. The Craft has its roots in a time when people lived in small communities, when communication and travel, over even small distances, were the exception rather than the rule. The village Witch was the nurse, doctor, midwife, vet and counsellor for the community. Witches were the ones who held the knowledge of healing and prepared the medicines of their time. They were the ones whose study of human actions and human nature enabled them to help their friends, family and neighbours solve their problems and resolve their differences. They were the ones whose observation of nature enabled them to advise on when to plant crops and when to harvest, and how best to treat and keep the animals which provided food for the months ahead. They cared for the people, the land, the growth and the future of their community. As keepers of knowledge, they also took the responsibility of selecting and training the next generation of healers and teachers.

Today's Witches often use the term 'near and dear' to refer to their community and, in a world where travel and communication are so much easier, this can extend to friends and Witches from far away. But the feeling is still that of family, whether through blood, fellowship in the Craft or simple friendship. The work is still that of healing, sharing knowledge and of caring for those in the immediate circle.

So what do Witches believe in and how do they practise the Craft? First, you have to understand that, unlike the more 'orthodox' religions, the Craft has no paid or formal priesthood; we are each our own Priest or Priestess and therefore make our own decisions as to the expression of our beliefs. As a result there is no 'one true way' to being a Witch. This gives rise to a great diversity in our daily practices and indeed enables the Craft to grow and adapt to the real world in a way that other paths find difficult because of their interpreted doctrine. Having said that, there are many beliefs and practices that most Witches hold in common:

WE BELIEVE THAT THE DIVINE IS BOTH MALE AND FEMALE. We believe this is equal and in balance, and that we should seek that balance in ourselves and in our lives. Speaking practically, we believe that there is a Goddess as well as a God, and that both are equally powerful, although some festivals and workings may be more appropriately directed to one or the other.

Both the Goddess and the God may be referred to by different names at different times, but this does not mean that each Witch believes that there are many Goddesses and many Gods. To illustrate this, think of a ball with many facets, similar to the kind seen at some concerts or discos. If each face of the ball is a different face of the Goddess or the God, there is still one ball, just as there is one Goddess and one God. If you were, say, working Magic with the aim of increasing your ability to study, you might wish to choose a different image, or facet, of the Goddess than you would if you were hoping to bring relief from illness for a friend.

We are each our own Priest or Priestess.

As mentioned above we have no formal priesthood in the Craft although those Witches working in a group or Coven (the name for a group of Witches) will have a High Priestess and High Priest who are the leaders of that group. This does not make them better Witches, it simply denotes their standing and authority within that group. Having no formal priesthood means we do not rely on others to interpret or intercede with our Gods for us, we are each entitled to make our

own connection with the Divine in our own way. This might be through ritual, meditation and/or Magic and most Witches will use a combination of different techniques at different times.

WE HAVE NO 'BOOK OF INSTRUCTION'.

We do not have a book in the way that Christians have the Bible or Muslims the Koran. There are a great number of books on the Craft, however, and it is up to those who wish to read some of these to make personal decisions as to their relevance. Each individual can choose the complexity of their rituals, and the form that their path will take. For some this may mean working in a group or Coven, others may prefer a Solitary path. Some will seek to work formalized Magic whilst others prefer the Hedgewitch approach, working closely with nature and using herbs to achieve their Magic.

EVERYONE IS ENTITLED TO THEIR OWN, INFORMED, CHOICE
OF SPIRITUAL PATH, SO LONG AS THEY HARM NO ONE.

Witchcraft is a non-proselytizing belief system – we do not feel the need for everyone to believe as we do in order to feel secure in our faith. There is plenty of room in this world for everyone to find their own way of relating to the Divine. In fact all religions have as much, if not more, in common than in difference. Hence there is no reason why we should not encourage and celebrate a diversity of beliefs. We encourage our young to examine many paths and to make their own decisions, based on their own needs. We do not seek to convert others to our beliefs, nor do we wish to be indoctrinated in turn.

WE BELIEVE THAT WE SHOULD RESPECT NATURE.
This means not taking more than we need and, indeed, trying to make recompense for that which we have taken. It involves trying to live not only in the modern

world but also in balance with the planet. Witches tend to shop second-hand, make at least some of the things they use and to recycle where they can. This does not mean that we are all 'green warriors' campaigning against the building of roads or houses. It does mean that we try to tread lightly on the world.

We utilize the elements in our workings.

It is not just that we respect nature, we also see ourselves reflected by the elements of Air, Fire, Water, Earth and Spirit. Whilst these elements are all around us in nature they are also within us: Air is our thoughts, Fire our passions and enthusiasm, Water our emotions, Earth our bodies and Spirit our inner selves. These are the energies we harness in working Magic and in order for this to be effective we must be able to achieve balance between them. These elements also have their reflections in daily life. For every project to work it must have its phases of thought, enthusiasm, emotional involvement and formation, and must also be imbued with its own spirit.

WE BELIEVE IN AND PRACTISE MAGIC.

Magic has been defined as the ability to create change by force of will and in some respects is not dissimilar to a belief in the power of prayer. However, in Magic it is our personal intervention which creates the change around us. Magic is not like cookery, just a matter of following a recipe and getting a result. True Magic requires a deep understanding of ourselves and the energies that are around us, and the ability to control and focus our own energies. One of the greatest keys to this is the ability to visualize. It also requires a study and understanding of the elements of Earth, Air, Fire and Water, not just in the world, but also within ourselves.

The Magic we practise is not that of stage conjuring or of the special effects that you see so often in modern films. It is practised to heal, protect and enhance our lives. It is worked for ourselves, our near and dear, and for those who come to us with requests for help. Magic should always be practised with the **Wiccan Rede** ('An' it harm none, do what thou will') in mind and also with regard to the **Law of Threefold Return** which states that whatever you do, good or ill, will be returned to you three times over. This latter is not confined to Magical working, but should be borne in mind at all times. If you are careful to harm no one and not to interfere with any-one's freedom of will, then you have the basic guidelines for good Magical practice.

WE PRACTISE DIVINATION.

Divination is the ability to find out things which might otherwise be hidden, whether that be the past, present, future or the presence of water or precious metals or minerals. It can be practised with or without tools such as the tarot, crystal ball, runes, tea-leaves or dowsing rods. It is referred to by many names, including fortune-telling, psychic reading, dowsing, and so on, although Witches will often use the somewhat older term of scrying. Nearly all Witches practise some form of divination. It is not a way of conjuring spirits who will answer questions, rather a way of accessing the inner mind to see what is coming up in our own and other people's lives.

WE CELEBRATE THE WHEEL OF THE YEAR.

The Witches' calendar contains eight key festivals, called Sabbats. At these we mark the changes of the seasons and the stories of the Goddess and the God. Whenever possible Witches will gather together to celebrate these festivals by dancing, singing and honouring the Goddess and the God by re-enacting their stories, but Solitary Witches also mark the Sabbats. At the end of these rituals we celebrate by feasting with food and wine. Many of the Sabbats have a familiar feel to non-Witches as they have been taken over by newer belief systems and incorporated into their calendars. We will discuss the

Sabbats, and how to celebrate them, in more detail in Chapter Four.

WE TAKE PERSONAL RESPONSIBILITY FOR OUR LIVES.

The main 'rule' in the Craft is called the **Wiccan Rede**: 'An' it harm none, do what thou will.' This in itself includes not only respect for others and the world around us, but also respect for ourselves. We believe that we cannot blame others for our thoughts, words and deeds, and that if we do wrong it is up to us to do our best to rectify it.

WE SEEK PERSONAL DEVELOPMENT.

There is much to learn in the world and in the Craft, but we do not expect others to feed us this information, we seek to expand our knowledge and extend our skills by personal effort. All Witches are aware that they will never know enough, let alone everything. This personal development also includes expanding our personal skills

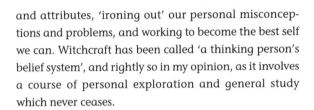

and attributes, 'ironing out' our personal misconceptions and problems, and working to become the best self we can. Witchcraft has been called 'a thinking person's belief system', and rightly so in my opinion, as it involves a course of personal exploration and general study which never ceases.

We believe in reincarnation.

Witches believe that we live many lives and between them we return to the Summerlands, a resting-place where we review the lessons we have learned in the life we have just completed and select the lessons to be learned in the life to come. When we speak of reincarnation we do not mean that we come back as the same person but rather that our spirit is born again. Whilst it can be interesting to research previous incarnations, and the information we acquire may illuminate aspects of our current lives, it is necessary to remember that the personal responsibility we also believe in means that we

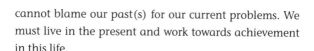

cannot blame our past(s) for our current problems. We must live in the present and work towards achievement in this life.

WE PRACTISE HERBLORE.

We utilize the properties of plants and nature for healing and self-improvement and in the course of our Magic. Herbs, plants and spices can be used in food and drink, lotions and ointments, sachets and talismans (Magical tokens), incense and candles. They can be used in their natural state (as I write this I have rosemary on my desk to aid my thoughts and concentration), fresh, dried or in the form of oil, as in aromatherapy, which has become so popular in recent years.

FROM GARDNERIANS TO SOLITARIES

Thus far I have only talked about Witches in general, but like many other belief systems there are many kinds of

Witch. The most commonly mentioned are Gardnerian, Alexandrian, Hereditary, Solitary and Hedgewitch. As you will see below, these categories are not necessarily exclusive; one can be Gardnerian Hereditary or Solitary Hedgewitch, or almost any other combination. There are those who do not fit into any of the above categories and there are those who have taken elements from outside the Craft to enrich their worship and their Magic.

Gerald Gardner is often termed 'the father of modern Witchcraft'. After the repeal of the Witchcraft Act in the 1950s, he was the first author and Witch to write about the Craft and to be relatively open about his involvement in it. Together with Doreen Valiente, he was responsible for some of the major elements of written Witchcraft that we have today. Gardnerians practise a lot of formalized ritual and quite a lot of working on the astral or psychic plane.

Alexandrian Craft is less formalized than Gardnerian. Alex Sanders came to prominence in the 1960s and 1970s when his flamboyant approach attracted a lot of public and media attention to the Craft, not all of it good! Alexandrian rituals can be adapted to suit people in many circumstances and in this way it is a more open and free-form religion.

Hedgewitches follow a more nature-based path and their rituals are often less formal than those of the Gardnerians or Alexandrians. Their Magic is often strongly connected with the use of herbs and plants, and frequently takes place in the open or in the kitchen.

Hereditary Witches, as the name implies, are those whose Craft is passed down through their family. Most Hereditaries are quite secretive, so that no one outside the family may realize they practise the Craft. Their rituals are closely-guarded family secrets and in some cases bear little resemblance to 'mainstream' or public Witchcraft.

Most of you reading this book, however, may find yourselves working as a Solitary. Solitaries may come from, and follow, any of the above paths, or even one of the lesser known ones. A great many Witches start by being Solitary, only joining a Coven when the right one comes along. Indeed, most people who follow the Craft will find themselves working as a Solitary at some time.

COVENS AND HOW THEY WORK

The Coven is the 'family group' of the Witches. It will usually be made up of a number of male and female Witches under the direction of the High Priestess and/or High Priest, although the High Priestess should have precedence.

The Coven will meet at the eight Sabbats and the 12 or 13 Full Moons. Some groups will also meet at the New Moon and this would make 33 meetings a year.

Outside meetings, members are expected to study their Craft and any specializations within it. They may also be assigned work by their High Priestess.

Group or Coven working is not always practical or

possible – it can be hard to find a group within reasonable travelling distance; it can be hard to find a group into which you fit, as it is important in group working that everyone feels comfortable with everyone else and that you can all work as a team, and it can be very hard to find the extra time which group work requires as you will need to be able to attend rituals at the times laid down by the High Priestess.

As I said earlier, many of you reading this book may find yourself working as a Solitary. Solitary working has a number of advantages and some disadvantages:

※ You do not need to go anywhere to do it. You can work in your bedroom, the garden or even a local park.

※ You can work whenever the need or mood takes you – you do not need much forward planning, although you still need to plan your Magic carefully.

However, you do not have the companionship and support of others who are following the same path and who may experience the same problems and difficulties.

 You have no one to share the joy of the Craft and your love of it. Whilst a Coven meeting is not a social activity, there is always time afterwards for celebration and laughter.

These latter two points can often be resolved, at least partly, by membership of a Pagan organization or through networking on the Internet.

CHAPTER THREE

THE GODDESS
AND THE GOD

'Known in many times, in many places

and by many names ...'

MOON WORSHIP?

One of the misconceptions about the Craft is that Witches worship the Moon –this is not so, though the Moon is significant to Witches because the phases of the Moon represent the aspects of the Goddess and because her consort, the God, is always with her. Witches utilize those phases in their worship and their working by timing their rituals and Magic to coincide with the phases of the Moon to which they will be most attuned.

The Moon has three major phases: waxing, full and waning. As the apparent size of the Moon changes, so does its influence on the Earth, and this is most clearly seen in its effects upon the tides. This influence can also be seen to affect humans, not surprisingly as we are mostly made of water. For women this link is easy to see in their monthly cycle, but everyone, male or female, is subject to monthly fluctuations in energy, patience, the ability to concentrate, and so on. These are often

referred to as biorhythms.

Early peoples from every civilization and every part of the world have, or had, stories to explain these changes in the Moon. All of these have certain threads in common. The Moon grows, bringing promise and strength. It reaches fullness, representing fertility and fruitfulness. It declines and then enters a resting, or hidden, phase for a few days before starting again. In the Craft these stages in the Moon's cycle are linked to the three aspects of the Triple Goddess – Maiden, Mother and Crone (or Wise One).

The **Maiden** is youthful. She represents fresh starts and new beginnings, enthusiasm and energy. In times past she would be seen as any woman who had commenced puberty but who had not yet given birth to a child. The Waxing Moon represents the Maiden and it is at this time of the month that we prefer to work Magic directed towards new growth or anything which is being started. It is the time to draw things towards us. So we would ask for help in starting a new project or job, or to acquire new skills. On a practical level it is a good time to sow seeds or start new plants.

The **Mother** is more mature. She represents fertility and fruitfulness, nurturing and caring. Her image is maternal, someone who has had a child (or children) and is in the process of raising them. The Full Moon represents the Mother and this is the time of month when our Magic is directed towards healing, nurturing and protecting.

The **Crone** is the Wise One. She represents knowledge and understanding. In times past this was the woman who had finished raising her family, whose experience of life and observation of the people around her had given her the knowledge and skill to know those things which were not obvious to others. The later stages of the Waning Moon represent the Crone and this is the time when Magic is worked towards knowledge and understanding, and when divination is most likely to be

successful. This is also the time for the banishing of things such as bad habits, old guilt, poor self-image. The Crone is also the one who presides over death, the time of rest after labours, and, because the cycle of life, death and rebirth is never-ending, she also prepares the way for new birth and the Maiden.

The few days when there is no visible Moon every month are called the Dark of the Moon. It is often considered that these nights, when the Goddess is hiding her face, are a time when no Magic should be performed. This is not strictly true, but working at the Dark of the Moon is something which should really be kept for emergencies and for when you are fully in tune with the energies in the ebb and flow of the Moon, otherwise you may find yourself working many times harder than is actually necessary, and with uncertain results.

So far I have referred to the cycle of the Moon only in terms of the Goddess; however we must remember that the God is of equal importance. He does not change in the same way with the phases of the Moon. His role is that of consort or partner and he remains constantly at the Goddess's side, changing little throughout the course of the month, although in a year of Moons there are some that are directly linked to the God. The aspects of the God are seen more clearly through the Wheel of the Year, where the Goddess sometimes appears to take a less obvious role. However, both the Goddess and the God are worshipped equally in both the Lunar and the annual cycles.

GODDESSES AND GODS

As I explained earlier, Witches refer to the Goddess and the God by a large number of different names and also as the Goddess and the God or the Lord and Lady, but this does not mean that each Witch believes that there are many Goddesses and Gods. (To help illustrate this earlier, I used the analogy of the mirror ball,

with each facet an aspect of the divine, known by a different name.)

The Gods and Goddesses known to Witches today come from a variety of pantheons and from a variety of times and lands. Knowledge of these deities has been spread by conquerors, invaders and immigrants throughout history and with today's global communication that knowledge is easily shared all around the world.

There is no way I can give a comprehensive list of Goddesses and Gods, their stories or their roles here, but the following are just a few to give you an introduction.

PERSEPHONE, DEMETER AND HECATE

This is just one example of the Triple Goddess. The story of Persephone's abduction by Pluto, Lord of the Underworld, is well known in its modern form but it is well worth researching the fuller tale, including the role of Hecate, who is the third aspect or Crone, and who is often called the Witches' Goddess.

Isis, Osiris, Nephtys and Set

These four Egyptian Goddesses and Gods are perhaps the best known of the Egyptian pantheon. Their story is one of those which have been changed and reinterpreted so that the 'villains' seem all bad and the 'heroes' all good. However, the full story is much more complex and contains all the ingredients of a soap opera! Nephtys is often invoked as a healer, particularly in more complicated or serious cases.

Venus and Aphrodite

Originally these were two quite different Goddesses. The Romans were the first to confuse their Goddess Venus with the Greek Aphrodite and both have come to represent love and beauty. Venus is often invoked by Witches who wish to work Magic for forms of self-love such as increased self-respect or personal emotional healing.

CERIDWYN

In the story of this Welsh Celtic Goddess, she devours Gwion, who has stolen the potion of inspiration which she has brewed in her Magical cauldron, and gives birth to the great poet and bard Taliesin. Ceridwyn, like Hecate, is also referred to as a Witches' Goddess.

CERNUNNOS

This Celtic God of the Hunt is one of several Gods often shown wearing antlers. Whilst his mythology is somewhat vague, a horned or antlered God is one of the older Gods of northern Europe.

THOR, ODIN, FREYA, FRIG AND LOKI

These Scandinavian Gods and Goddesses and many others share a vast mythology which is often referred to as the Northern Tradition. Whilst this tradition has much in common with Witchcraft, it is often considered to be a different path.

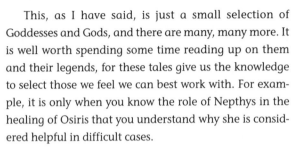

This, as I have said, is just a small selection of Goddesses and Gods, and there are many, many more. It is well worth spending some time reading up on them and their legends, for these tales give us the knowledge to select those we feel we can best work with. For example, it is only when you know the role of Nepthys in the healing of Osiris that you understand why she is considered helpful in difficult cases.

Most Witches have their 'favourite' deity or deities. These will be the ones with whom they most closely identify and may even be the ones to whom they dedicate themselves and their Witchcraft. These Gods and/or Goddesses may come from one pantheon or from a mixture, but it is usual to stay within any one pantheon during the course of any one working and not mix, say, a Greek Goddess with a Celtic God, as these deities will not necessarily be in sympathy with each other and the energies they produce may cancel each other out.

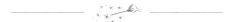

Many Witches like to have an image of the Goddess and the God on their Altar when working Magic and even just around the house generally. This can be a statue, a picture or drawing, or some other symbol. One of the easiest ways to do this is to purchase a postcard from a museum or copy an illustration from a book. It is not necessary to have an image of each and every Goddess or God you wish to work with, but it can be very helpful to have something around which aids your focus.

Witches do not always refer to the Goddess and the God by any name at all. Some prefer only to talk about the Goddess and the God, or even to refer to them as the Lady and the Lord. In this case the images they may keep around them may be fairly simple – a round stone with a hole through it to represent the Goddess, a phalli-cally shaped stone to represent the God, for example. Of course, two things which represent the Goddess and the God and which are present at most rituals are the Chalice and the Athame (the Witches' knife).

CHAPTER FOUR

CELEBRATING THE WHEEL
OF THE YEAR

'Ye shall dance, sing, feast ...

all in my name ...'

Samhain: 31 October

Yule: 21 December

Imbolg: 2 February

Oestara: 21 March

Beltane: 1 May

Litha: 21 June

Lammas: 1 August

Madron: 21 September

Witches celebrate eight seasonal festivals called the Sabbats. Taken together, they form the Wheel of the Year. At these festivals Witches celebrate the seasons, the agricultural cycle of sowing, growing and reaping, and the cycle of the Goddess and the God.

Almost certainly the dates of these festivals, as celebrated today, are not the same as the ones that would have been celebrated before the arrival of the structured calendar and the universal system of counting the passage of time. The Major Sabbats of Samhain, Imbolg,

Beltane and Lammas would have been timed by observing what actually happened in the world around. Hence Imbolg would have been celebrated when the first lambs were born, Beltane when the May came into bloom, Lammas when the first harvest was ready and Samhain when it was obvious that no more could be gathered before the winter storms. The Lesser Sabbats of Yule, Oestara, Litha and Madron all relate to the passage of the Sun, being the Winter and Summer Solstices and the Spring and Autumn Equinoxes. It is likely that these would have been celebrated two or three days after the actual event, when it was possible for people to have observed the changing length of day and night.

It is often said by modern Witches that the Sabbats are a time for celebration, not a time for Magical working, and this is a valid point of view. Magic, the work of Witches, can be performed at all the phases of the Moon, hence time for reflection on the passage of the year and for celebrating the cycles of the Goddess and

the God should be set aside. However, the tides of energy are very strong at the Sabbats and sometimes it can be appropriate to perform Magical working at these times. This is not to say that you must perform Magic at every Sabbat, nor is it a good idea to save your Magical workings for them, as many problems simply cannot be left until the appropriate Sabbat comes around. Also, many can be solved without the added energy of a Sabbat.

So, how do Witches celebrate the Sabbats? The celebration can take many forms, depending on the circumstances of the individual, but for those who are part of a Coven, these are times for getting together, and each of the Sabbats will be marked by a ritual followed by a feast.

Witches who work on their own, whether through choice or necessity, may perform rituals or choose less obvious ways of celebrating the Wheel of the Year. I worked as a Solitary for many years and have celebrated the festivals with anything from work done in the garden to silent meditation on a walk through the woods.

There is not space in this book to include specific rituals for marking each Sabbat (there are many excellent books available on this subject), but in the following pages you will find some general suggestions for celebrating each Sabbat, including some ideas should you wish to share the seasonal celebration with friends or family. (This is not as an opportunity to preach or convert, but simply as a way of sharing the seasonal feeling). Once you understand the content and meaning of the festivals you can devise your own ways of marking them meaningfully for yourself.

People living in the Southern Hemisphere will find their seasons are reversed and may prefer to celebrate the Sabbats as appropriate to the season rather than the calendar date.

SAMHAIN

31 OCTOBER

Most usually pronounced 'Sow'ain', this is the most important festival of the Witch's year. Samhain marks the beginning and the end of the Wheel of the Year in the same way that New Year does in the conventional calendar.

In the agricultural cycle this was a time when people gave a long hard look at what they had to last them through the cold days of winter. They would slaughter and salt down any animals that they felt either wouldn't make it through the winter or which they couldn't afford to support on the stocks from the harvest. So Samhain was a major feast and often the last time some fresh foods, especially meat, would be eaten until new life started again in spring.

The themes of this festival are: the end of the old year and start of the new; a time when the veil between

the worlds of the living and the dead is at its thinnest and spirits can roam; a time of remembering those we have loved who have gone before; a time of looking forward and of scrying and divination (trying to see what will come).

At this time the Goddess takes on her robes of Crone and the God becomes the Hunter who will lead the Wild Hunt throughout the winter.

CELEBRATING SAMHAIN

✳ Wait until the first very cold or even frosty day which marks this season (if you are in the Southern Hemisphere then you will need some other seasonal marker) and go for a walk. Look at nature and reflect upon the changes you see, the signs of life as well as the signs that a period of the year is over. Think about the way these changes are reflected in your own life. In doing so you will find yourself closer to the natural cycle of life, death and rebirth.

Remember that in nature, death and decay are just a natural resting point before new life and new growth.

※ As this is a festival of death, it is a good time to remember those who have gone before, not in a melancholy way but by laying particular emphasis on the things you shared and the achievements of that person. There are many ways to do this – look through old photographs and remember the good times, make a visit to someone's burial site or to a location you shared together, read their favourite book or poem, or listen to a piece of music you enjoyed together.

YULE

21 DECEMBER

This is the Winter Solstice, the point at which the hours of daylight stop decreasing and start to lengthen. The

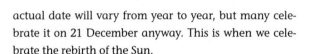

actual date will vary from year to year, but many celebrate it on 21 December anyway. This is when we celebrate the rebirth of the Sun.

At Yule, the Oak King, Lord of the Summer, is reborn. In legend the Oak and Holly Kings are brothers who share the rule of the year, with the Oak King reigning from midwinter to midsummer, the period of increasing light, and the Holly King reigning from midsummer to midwinter, the period of increasing darkness. At the Solstices, light and dark are said to battle to determine which will have control over the coming months and many Covens will re-enact the fight between the Oak and Holly Kings, making sure, of course, that the 'right' King wins.

CELEBRATING YULE

✶ Rising before dawn to greet the Sun is one way of celebrating this festival, but it is not for the faint-hearted in midwinter. We often follow this with a

very non-traditional 'feast' of fried egg-and-bacon sandwiches washed down with hot chocolate laced with brandy. Not exactly health food, but definitely a warming reward for rising early enough to climb somewhere to see the Sun's first appearance over the horizon.

✳ To mark this Sabbat many people will prepare a Yule Log. This is normally a real log, onto which you place a number of candles, one for everyone who will be present. Get each person in your group or family to light a candle, representing the return of the days of increasing light, and express a wish for the forthcoming season. Traditionally the Yule Log would then be retained until the following year, when it would be placed in the hearth and allowed to burn.

IMBOLG

2 FEBRUARY

Now we see the first signs of life returning to the land, the first buds on the trees, the first flowers peeking through the frozen earth. The sheep are in lamb and in some areas the first lambs have already been born, so we know that spring will come again. At this time the Goddess changes from Crone to Maiden, full of hope and promise of life to come, and we celebrate her return with candles, hence the more modern Candlemas. The God, who was reborn at Yule, is now seen as a young man full of vigour, and his pursuit of the Maiden starts at this Sabbat.

CELEBRATING IMBOLG

✳ As this is a time of new life and growth, it is appropriate to plant bulbs or   flowers or to sow seeds. You may, however, have to wait a week (or several) until the last frosts have passed.

 If you are lucky enough to live near a suitable tree, choose one to be 'your own'. This is the tree that you will watch to mark the seasons. Observe its cycles of growth and fruitfulness, the way it reacts to the seasons. By doing this you will have a natural link to the Wheel of the Year. There are many trees which have particular significance to Witches: oak, ash, hawthorn, elder, willow, rowan and many others.

OESTARA

21 MARCH

This is the festival of the Anglo-Saxon Dawn Goddess Eostar (also known as Eostra or Ostara). Her symbols are the egg and the hare, which was later softened to the rabbit in modern festivals. Eostar is a Goddess of Fertility and this is a festival not just of fertility of the body and the land, but also of the mind, of hopes and

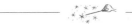

wishes. This was traditionally a time when the first seeds would be sown.

It is also the Spring (or Vernal) Equinox, when day and night, light and dark, are equal, and it is this balance that we seek in our lives. It is the time when we turn out the old (the origins of spring cleaning) and take on the new. In the Craft we do this in terms of casting off old fears and worries, outworn guilt and completed projects, and taking on new hopes and aspirations. Just as the land is celebrating a rebirth, so do we in our personal lives.

CELEBRATING OESTARA

※ Celebrate the arrival of spring with flowers. Bring them into your home and, in keeping with the theme of balance, give them to others.

※ A game greatly loved by the young is the egg hunt. This can take place indoors or out. Make sure that

you have plenty of small eggs, some well hidden
and some easy to find for the very small.

BELTANE

1 MAY

Beltane is the second most important festival of the year.
The Goddess sheds her robes of Maiden and takes on
those of Mother, the God casts aside the irresponsibility of
youth and takes his place as her consort, and we celebrate their marriage. Beltane is a fertility festival and it
used to be that all the unattached men and women
would dress in green and spend the night in the woods
seeking a partner. Children born as a result of May eve
were considered to be especially blessed, as they were
considered children of the God. This tradition then
became celebrated in the choosing of a May Queen, who
then selected her partner the May King, and the two
presided over the May celebrations. These celebrations

would also include dancing around the Maypole, another fertility ritual which is still being revived in Britain after Cromwell banned it in the seventeenth century.

In keeping with the marriage of the Goddess and God, many modern Witches and Pagans will celebrate their wedding, or Handfasting as it is called, at this time.

Celebrating Beltane

✳ As this festival celebrates the marriage of the Goddess and the God it really is the time for a major feast, a wedding supper. Roast pork is a good meat for this festival, served traditional style with all the trimmings and of course a good home-made apple sauce.

✳ If you are fortunate, you may well find a May Day celebration taking place near you, perhaps Maypole dancing, Morris dancing or a May fair. Beltane was always a time when the whole community would

join together to celebrate the onset of summer and being with others reminds us of the continuity of our beliefs.

LITHA

21 JUNE

This is the Summer Solstice. From this point onwards the hours of daylight will decrease in length and the hours of darkness increase. This is the height of the Sun's power and in the Northern Hemisphere summer itself really begins at this time. At this point the battle of Oak and Holly is once more enacted, only this time Lord Oak gives way to Lord Holly.

The Goddess at this time of the year is still wearing her robes of Mother and she is full of the promise of harvest.

Celebrating Litha

🌟 Try to find some way of being outside for this Sabbat, or at least part of it. You may be able to rise at dawn to greet the Sun, but if not, take a walk during part of the day and use this time to observe the cycle of growth and decline. Many plants have already given their best for the year and will be dying back to make room for others. Reflect on the things in your own life which have run their course and which should now be replaced by new growth.

🌟 Hold a midsummer party. Give it themes of yellow and gold for the Sun's peak and dark and light green for the battle of the Oak and Holly Lords. It may be possible for you to have a mock battle in honour of the Oak and Holly Kings, but if you can't, don't let this spoil your enjoyment of the party or the festival.

LAMMAS

1 AUGUST

This is the festival of the first of the harvest and as such would have been a time of great rejoicing. Whole communities, men, women and children together, would have gathered to harvest the crops and to celebrate afterwards. Lammas has also been called 'loaf-mass', which is a reminder of just how important the first grain and its bread were.

The main themes of Lammas are the death and rebirth of the God, the festival of Lugh the Sun God and of the Corn King (who is still represented by the gingerbread man), the first harvest and personal sacrifice to repay what we have been given.

Whereas other Sabbats are sometimes about giving up the old to take on the new, Lammas is concerned with making sure we have given enough for what we have received.

CELEBRATING LAMMAS

✳ Make your own gingerbread men and share them amongst your friends and family. If you are a good cook, or feeling adventurous, you might also like to make your own Lammas Loaf, plaited into the shape of a wheatsheaf or in the form of a man.

✳ Make a sacrifice of time and effort for the land around you or the community you live in, for example, you could go to a local park or the woods to collect litter. We make a family day of this, adults and children working alongside each other and competing to see who can fill the most sacks with rubbish. After we have disposed of this we have a party where we share our Lammas loaf and gingerbread men.

MADRON

21 SEPTEMBER

This is the Autumn Equinox, when day and night, light and dark, are equal. It is the feast at the height of the harvest, when nearly all has been gathered in. This would have been a time of markets, festivals, processions and general gaiety. It is also known as the feast of the healer and the feast of the release of prisoners, for this is a time of year for setting aside old disputes, grudges and quarrels. Like the Spring Equinox it is a time of balance, a time to discard unwanted habits and traits and to take on new.

CELEBRATING MADRON

⚹ Find a symbol of balance. This could be something man-made, such as a Yin-Yang symbol or even a set of scales, the old-fashioned kind with two arms. Alternatively, it could be something from nature such as a stone which is both light and dark in colour. Whatever the item, place it somewhere where you will be easily able to see it. This is a reminder not just of the balance of the Equinox, but also of the balance which we seek in our lives all year round.

✳ If you can find 'common land' which supports fruit, berries and nuts, try taking the whole family on a ramble. Take your field guide with you and expand your knowledge of what is available in your area. Obviously you should never eat anything you are not sure of, although few poisonous species taste pleasant enough for you to persevere to the point of making yourself ill.

CHAPTER FIVE

BECOMING A WITCH

'As is my will so mote it be'

It might seem that becoming a Witch is very complicated, but in essence it is no more complicated than
deciding to become, say, a Christian. If you think of the
Craft as being in three parts – religion, ritual and Magic
– then those can be looked at as three distinct steps.
First, if you feel that the tenets and beliefs of the Witch
are for you (as discussed in Chapter Two), then you can
start being a Witch from that point. The second step is
working the Craft. It will take you time to understand
the various rituals and to formulate your preferred way
of performing them, but the guidelines in Chapters
Seven and Eight will help you there. Magic, the third
step, will take longer to understand, and will require
study and practice before you will get it right. The good
news is that failed Magic rarely does any harm – it simply doesn't work.

As I said above, if the beliefs of the Witch give a good
indication of your spiritual beliefs, then you are already
in a position to call yourself Witch if you wish. However,

many people feel that simply 'applying the label' is not enough, they want to make some formal declaration. In a Coven this involves a process called three degrees of initiation; for someone working on their own this is called self-initiation or, more correctly, self-dedication, and this is what we are going to look at here.

SELF-DEDICATION

Working as a Solitary you can perform a ritual of self-dedication to mark your choice of path. This can be as simple or as elaborate as you wish. The one below is quite simple, but you can always add to it.

Many individuals choose to take a Witch name at this time. A Witch name does not have to be the name of a Goddess or God; indeed, to choose the name of a major deity is overly arrogant. Try not to be too obvious. The Craft and Paganism in general are in danger of being overrun by those called Raven, Morrigan, Willow,

Morgan and Merlin. You might choose the name of a herb, plant or tree, a country, sea or river, an animal, bird or fish, a mythical place or creature.

Working on your own you do not need robes, whether plain or elaborate, but many people like to choose an item of clothing or jewellery which they will set aside for their Craft work. This can be a special shirt or dress, a ring or necklace, or anything else which you feel meets your need to mark the change from being your everyday self to being a working Witch.

At this point you also need to give some thought as to how you actually perceive the divine. Do you wish to call upon the Goddess and the God by name, or as the Lord and Lady? If by name, which names? You can of course refer to them as the Lord and Lady most of the time and only use specific deities and titles when they are appropriate to your rites. But if you are intending to dedicate yourself to a specific deity or deities then you should

read up on their stories and be able to visualize them clearly in your mind's eye.

Write your own promise of dedication. There is one included in the following ritual and you are welcome to alter it for your own use, but often it is better if you make up your own words, as a good part of the effectiveness of any ritual comes from the knowledge that your words reflect your intentions precisely.

You will need to set a date for your ritual. Obviously you can choose one of the Sabbats, but you may find that you have to wait a while before your preferred date comes around. Either the Full Moon or New Moon are excellent times for self-dedication. Alternatively you can select a date which has special significance to your chosen deities.

THE RITUAL OF SELF-DEDICATION

PREPARATION

As with all rites and rituals, the first thing is preparation. Select your working space with care. It needs to be somewhere where you can rely on being undisturbed. It does not need to be large, but you should have a small work area which can be cleared to serve as your Altar. Ideally this should be in the north of the room. Your room should be clean and tidy. Think of it this way – you are dedicating yourself to the Craft and to the Goddess and the God, and you do not want to invite them to a pigsty, do you?

Gather together everything you will be using in your ritual and make sure that this is also clean. Have your promise of self-dedication written out clearly and to hand. Ideally, you should commit as much of your ritual to heart as possible, but we all feel nervous and forget our 'lines' from time to time.

Don't forget to prepare yourself. If you can, take a bath and wash your hair. Whilst you bathe, meditate on what you are about to do and also on the Goddess and the God.

What You Will Need
(Chapter Seven contains more information about the following tools, as well as a list of substitutions if you cannot use any of them.)

Altar: If you are working on the floor you might like to use a scarf or silk square to denote your Altar area.

Two candles: One each for the Lord and the Lady. Tea lights are quite good enough. Don't forget the matches.

Incense: A single incense stick is enough. Frankincense, jasmine and sandalwood are all good choices.

Water: In a small bowl or dish.

Salt: A very small amount in a dish or saucer.

Wine: A Chalice or small glass of wine.

Athame or wand: If you do not yet have one you can use your right index finger.

Your working clothing or jewellery.

Your notes.

THE RITUAL

Having prepared yourself and cleared a small area to work in, check again to ensure you are not likely to be disturbed. Do not yet put on your working clothing or jewellery. Place everything you will need onto your Altar, leaving a working area in the centre.

Stand, kneel or sit in front of your Altar and with your eyes closed, take several deep slow breaths. Take your time, feel yourself relax and when you are ready you can open your eyes.

Now light your incense and, holding your hands one to each side of it, say: *'I call upon the element of Air to watch over me, to guard, guide and protect me during these my rites. Blessed Be.'* Strongly visualize the element – think of cool breezes and strong winds. When you are sure you can see it in your mind's eye you can move on to the next element.

Light one candle and again holding your hands to the sides of it so they will not get burnt, say: *'I call upon the element of Fire to watch over me, to guard, guide and protect me during these my rites. Blessed Be.'* This time you can see the flame of the candle. Visualize fire, flames and a volcano erupting.

Hold your hands over the water and say: *'I call upon the element of Water to watch over me, to guard, guide and protect me during these my rites. Blessed Be.'* Visualize rivers, streams and the oceans.

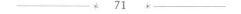

Hold your hands palms downwards over the salt and say: *'I call upon the element of Earth to watch over me, to guard, guide and protect me during these my rites. Blessed Be.'* While you are doing this, visualize the element of Earth: rocks, stones, soil, etc.

Next, light the second candle from the first and, holding your hands upwards to each side of the Altar, visualize the Goddess and the God. Sometimes it can help to close your eyes to do this. Take your time and when you are happy that you can feel them with you, say: *'I welcome the Lord and Lady [use their names if this is what you have decided to do]. I ask them to be with me, to watch over me and to witness my Rite of Self-Dedication.'* Now you need to read or speak your promise, for example: *'I, [your usual name], call upon the Old Gods and the elements of Earth, Air, Fire and Water to witness that I have, of my own free will, chosen the path of the Witch. I dedicate myself and all my works to the service of the Goddess and the God. I promise that I will not use the Craft, or the knowledge I gain, to impress the foolish or to*

frighten the childish. I promise to uphold the Craft and the Wiccan Rede to the best of my ability and to keep silent about the secrets I may learn and the knowledge I may gain.'

If you have chosen a new name, now is the time to make that part of your promise: *'In token of my promise I take to myself the name of [Witch name] that I may grow in its likeness. May the Old Ones know me by this name and may I always be faithful to it.'* Whether or not you have chosen a new name, you should now dedicate your special clothing or jewellery: *'I dedicate this [name the item] to my Craft work and to the service of the Old Ones, that it may always remind me of this my sacred promise.'* Take the item and pass it quickly through the incense smoke: *'I dedicate it with Air.'* Pass it very quickly over the flame: *'I dedicate it with Fire.'* Sprinkle it with a little water: *'I dedicate it with Water.'* Sprinkle it with a little salt: *'I dedicate it with Earth.'* Then, holding it up over the Altar: *'And I offer it and my love to the Lord and the Lady. Blessed Be.'* Now you can put the item on.

Next take the Chalice of wine and your Athame. Holding the Chalice in both hands, say: *This is the Chalice, symbol of the Goddess, the Great Mother who brings love and fruitfulness to us all.* Place the Chalice back onto your Altar and take your Athame in both hands, point facing upwards: *This is the Athame, symbol of the Horned God.* Now transfer the Athame to your right (or strong) hand, holding it point downwards, and take the Chalice in your other hand. Insert the tip of the Athame into the wine and say: *'Joined together they bring forth life eternal.'*

Remove the Athame from the Chalice and replace it on the Altar. Place both hands around the Chalice and hold it high over the Altar towards the Goddess and the God. Take a small sip of the wine and say: *'In perfect love and perfect trust. Blessed Be.'* Then replace the Chalice on the Altar.

Dip the forefinger of your right (or strong) hand into the wine, anoint yourself in the centre of your forehead and say: *'With this wine, consecrated by the Goddess and the God, I anoint myself in earnest of the promise I have made this day.*

May the Old Ones watch over me, guard me, guide me and protect me in my new and chosen path. Blessed Be.' Now take just a few moments to reflect upon the promise you have made, perhaps having another sip or two of your wine.

When you are ready, you can now clear away. First thank the Goddess and the God. Hold your hands high over the Altar, visualize them and say: *'I, [new Witch name], give thanks to the Lord and Lady for attending and witnessing these rites. Blessed Be.'* Next hold your hands over, or beside, each of the elements in turn, as you did when invoking them, and say: *'I give thanks to thee, O element of Earth [Air, Fire, Water], for attending and witnessing these rites. Blessed Be.'* As you do so, visualize each element departing or fading in your mind.

Once all has been cleared away on the psychic or astral plane, you should clear away on the material plane. Restore your room to its original state – although if it was untidy then you do not need to untidy it again! Put

your special item of clothing or jewellery away somewhere safe. Clean all your working tools and restore them to their correct places.

After your ritual and clearing away it is a good idea to ground yourself. During ritual or working, your spiritual self becomes uplifted and it needs to be literally brought down to Earth again. One of the best ways of doing this is to eat and drink something. This is why so many rituals and celebrations end with feasting.

PART 2:

SPELLCRAFT

CHAPTER SIX

WORKING
SUCCESSFUL MAGIC

'Magic is the ability to create change

by force of will'

Magic is often defined as 'the ability to create change by force of will'. It is not about blindly following a series of instructions, reciting the 'right' words or having the right ingredients, like baking a cake. It is about harnessing and controlling your own will, or power of mind, to create the change you seek.

It's important to remember that there is a difference between working Magic and performing a ritual. Rituals can be used to celebrate the Sabbats, to honour the Gods, to give thanks for Magic successfully completed and for many other things which are not of themselves Magic. Magic is an act, or acts, which may be contained within ritual, although Magic can also be practised outside ritual. There are some traditions within the Craft which disapprove of working Magic outside formal ritual, but, as almost every Witch knows, there are times when your circumstances will not allow for a great deal of formality.

CASTING THE CIRCLE

The first ritual that almost every Witch learns is that of creating the Sacred Space. As I've mentioned earlier, Witches do not usually have temples or even rooms set aside which are the equivalent of their 'church', instead they create their Sacred Space wherever and whenever they need it. The full or formal way of doing this would be to consecrate the elemental symbols on the Altar, invoke the elements, invite the Lord and Lady and cast the Circle. These actions are often jointly referred to as 'casting the Circle'. Once the Circle is cast, the contents of the ritual will vary, but frequently they will include Drawing Down the Moon, where the High Priest invokes the Goddess into the High Priestess; some form of power raising, maybe dance and chant; the centre, or object, of the ritual, an act of Magic or a rite of passage such as a Handfasting perhaps; the Rite of Wine and Cakes or the Great Rite; a blessing, usually given by the High Priestess.

The Circle is closed by banishing the elements, thanking the Lord and Lady and removing the Circle itself. Feasting may take place either just before or just after the Circle is closed.

As you can see, just casting and later removing the Circle can be quite an involved process and whilst working steadily through all these steps is an excellent way of bringing together a group of people, there are simpler ways of working if you are on your own. We'll be looking at a method of creating the Sacred Space in the next chapter (see pages 109–14).

But first let us just quickly look at the purpose behind casting a Circle and each of the steps involved in it. The main reasons are to protect those working in it and to provide a way of containing the energies (or power) raised for Magical working until you are ready to release it.

The Altar will have been laid with a cloth of the colour appropriate to the season or purpose of the ritual. On it will be all the items which are to be used within the ritual, including incense to represent Air, a candle to represent Fire, a bowl of water to represent the element of Water, and salt to represent Earth. (On pages 100–109 you will find a list of Magical substitutions so that you can find ways around using anything which may cause a problem with those around you.) Each of these elemental symbols will have to be consecrated and purified, excepting salt which is deemed to be pure in itself and therefore needs only blessing. There will also be a statue or symbol of the Goddess and the God, and/or a candle or candles dedicated to them. There will be a chalice of wine and a plate of cakes for the Rite of Wine and Cakes, together with your Athame, unless you wear it at your belt. Unless the Altar cloth has one embroidered on it, there will be an Altar pentagram, symbolizing the combination and balance of the four elements together with the fifth, Spirit, which you your-self bring to the Circle. In addition to all of this there will also be the items needed for the working of whatever

Magic you intend to do within the ritual, or, in the case of celebrating a Sabbat, symbols of that festival.

The purpose of most of the items is to provide a visual key, so that when everyone in the group sees them they tune into the same thing. For example, suppose I say to a group of people, 'Visualize a cup,' one person may think about their favourite coffee mug, another may think of a golden chalice, and so on. However, if I hold my chalice up in front of them and say, 'See this cup,' everyone will be thinking of the same thing. Now, if I am working on my own, I do not actually need the cup at all, unless I am planning to put something into it.

THE KEYS TO EFFECTIVE MAGIC

The observant amongst you will by now have noticed that most of the items on the Altar and most of the steps in casting a Circle fall into two categories: **the elements** and **the Goddess and the God**. These are two of the keys

to working Magic, but when working alone we do not need to have visible or physical representations to remind us because they are all around us and they are within us. The Goddess and the God are day and night, light and dark, summer and winter, and can be seen in the cycle of the Moon and the Wheel of the Year. They are also our female and male attributes. The elements, too, relate to things in the world around us and within us, as follows:

Air: spring, morning, the direction of east, the colour yellow, the air we breathe, the winds around us, youth and new beginnings, and our thoughts. One of the reasons why, when calling upon the elements, we start with Air is because thought should always take place before action!

Fire: summer, afternoon, south, red, the Sun that warms and lights us, maturity and our passions or enthusiasms.

Water: autumn, evening, west, blue, the rain, rivers and oceans, middle age, our emotions.

Earth: winter, night, north, green, the rocks, stones and earth we walk upon, old age, wisdom, our physical self and our actions. (North is also considered to be the direction of power for Witches. This is one of the reasons why the Altar is often placed in the north.)

These links are called correspondences and there are many of them. Particular Gods and Goddesses, scents, sounds, other colours, animals, birds, and so on, can all be linked to each other. Correspondences are not just attached to the elements – you can find tables of them associated with almost anything. However, whilst it is a good idea to have a look at these if you can, you do not need to commit them to memory or to follow them slavishly. It is far better to start with the basics and then add your own, as your own links or associations will have far more meaning, and hence power, for you.

Understanding the elements, accepting their place within us and in life, and working towards a balance between them is one of the main features in being able to work Magic.

Once you have explored the elements and come to understand how they feel to you, then you can begin to summon those forces from within yourself, without the need for a lot of tools or equipment as visual reminders. But before you get to this stage you may need to have some small reminders before you on your Altar, or just around you when you work.

I mentioned above that the elements, and the Goddess and the God, were two of the keys to working effective Magic. The third is **visualization**. To visualize is to be able to imagine something and hold that image in your mind's eye as strongly as if it were there in front of you. For some people this comes fairly easily, but most people find that they have to work quite hard and prac-

tise regularly to be able to form a picture and hold it in place for any length of time. Again, this is where the use of physical links comes in. If, say, you are working a healing Magic for Ann, then it is a lot easier to visualize Ann getting better if you have a picture of her to work with.

The next key to successful Magic is **knowledge**. Still using the example of healing Ann, it will be easier to work the healing Magic if you understand exactly what is wrong with her and how the physical process of healing might take place. Suppose she has a broken leg, you can visualize the bone knitting together and becoming whole again. If she has an infected finger, you can visualize her white blood cells rushing to the site to remove infection. This is not to say that you cannot simply visualize Ann getting well, but that your Magic will be that much easier to direct if you know exactly where to send it and what it is to do when it gets there. Of course knowledge also means that you need to be precise about what you are working towards.

WHY MAGIC SOMETIMES DOESN'T WORK

One of the commonest causes of Magic 'going wrong' is not deciding exactly what it is you are trying to do. One of the sayings in the Craft is 'Be careful what you wish for', as you just might get it! In other words, you might get what you asked for, rather than what you wanted. For example, say you want to be noticed by someone who attracts you. Next day you might find your trousers get covered in pink paint. The Gods have a sense of humour too!

Likewise, if you just ask for money you may find that you find a penny on the ground, or that your favourite aunt dies and leaves it to you in her will, or that your car is written off in an accident and whilst you get the insurance money, you still have to buy a new car. It is usually recommended that if you want money it is best to ask for the opportunity to earn it. This is not just a moral issue,

there are reasons for it. First, the concept of money is not one which exists in nature, and the Craft is about working with nature and natural forces. Secondly, all Magic involves an exchange of energies – you cannot create something out of nothing – but work for cash is in itself an exchange and therefore Magic is more likely to succeed.

Another reason for Magic not working is a lack of belief on the part of the person working it that the Magic either can or should work. Put more simply, there are some things that we 'just know' cannot be achieved through Magic and there are others which, deep down inside, we believe it is wrong to do. For example, in the first case, very few people are prepared to believe that they can change the wheel on a car by Magic. In the second case, we all know that it would be wrong to kill someone, whether by Magic or any other method. In both these cases the Magic will fail.

There is another, very important, reason for Magic not working: some things are just not meant to be. This is often the case with trying to heal those who are terminally ill, as when it is time for a person to move on from this world, nothing can change that. This is something which many people find very hard to accept. However, we have to realize that often the loss of someone we love is something which might be best for them, even though it may pain us a great deal.

AREAS FOR MAGICAL WORKING TO CONSIDER CAREFULLY

In fact working **healing** of any kind is something which needs a great deal of thought. If you remove someone's pain when they have a broken bone, it may result in them using that part and aggravating the injury. If you work for longer life for someone who is dying, it may result in them lingering in great pain. So you need to consider very carefully what you are going to do and all the possible 'side effects' it may have. One of these

which should not be underestimated is that many people will go to a Witch for physical healing and then 'forget' to go to the doctor too! Obviously, the responsible Witch will always ask about, or suggest, conventional medicine as well. Often when working Magic for the seriously ill, the best method is simply to ask the Goddess to care for them and for all those around them. In this way you can leave the decision to the divine, rather than playing Goddess (or God) yourself.

Another really tricky area for Magical intervention is that of **relationships**, whether your own or someone else's. On a personal front, however much in love you are with someone, would you really be happy if you thought that it was your Magic that attracted them? Well you might at first, but in a few weeks or months you would be wondering if they really liked you or if they were just with you because of a spell you worked. If you find yourself contemplating this sort of Magic, then it is better to consider things like arranging an opportunity

to meet or increasing your own self-confidence.

Working Magic for other people's relationships is even more fraught with complications. First, you have to realize that this is an area where you might be interfering with someone's freedom of will. Secondly, you are entering an area where you can never have all the information or enough knowledge. Say someone comes to you asking you to repair their broken marriage. You almost certainly will not know the whole story, as any one individual can only give their perception of the way things are. Quite frankly, even if you can assume that they are trying to be totally honest, they will not know what is, or has been, going on in their partner's life, let alone their mind. There may already be another partner, even a family, in existence, and to work Magic to bring the leaving person back might wreck the lives of other people. Also, you can never be sure of the 'rights and wrongs' of any situation involving two people and their emotions, as it is almost certain that you will only

be given one person's point of view. You cannot know just how irritating, or even unreasonable, even your best friend might be to live with! In these cases I usually play safe by arranging for the couple to have an opportunity to communicate with each other. In this way if the relationship is revivable, then they have the chance, and even if it isn't, an opportunity to talk rarely harms.

Sooner or later nearly everyone is also tempted to do **hexes, curses and revenge spells**. I cannot tell you not to do these. Just one thing to bear in mind, though: however just your actions may seem to you, you must be prepared for that negative energy to rebound on you, or someone close to you, three times over.

If you really must get your own back on someone, the best curse of all is simply to ask that they 'get what they truly deserve'. In this way, you can leave it to the Goddess to decide on the rights and wrongs of the situation and what, if any, action needs to be taken. Remember also that working negative Magic is very much against the Wiccan Rede: 'An' it harm none, do what thou will.' Besides, I've always found that annoying and irritating people, if left to their own devices, reap the rewards of their behaviour eventually, and the nastier they are, the more quickly it tends to happen.

One other main category of Magical working is that of **protection**. These days it seems that an increasing number of people feel under threat or attack. This may be physically, from an angry ex-lover for example, or psychically, either from someone working Magic against them, or from some form of 'entity' they believe to be around.

Anyone who feels subject to the threat of physical attack should be encouraged to take practical measures to counter this – improve their security, report it to the police or even move house. But there are Craft measures that can also be taken. Bearing in mind that cursing is not a good option, one of the better measures is to work towards the aggressor moving away, perhaps by doing a

spell to get them an irresistible job offer a long way off.

In cases of perceived psychic attack, you need to know that this is in reality very rare. However, it is one of the symptoms of some kinds of mental illness. Obviously you cannot suggest this to your friend or client without the risk of causing huge offence, but do be cautious in your judgement of anyone who comes to you seeking protection from an 'outside force'. There are a number of Craft measures that can be taken against negativity, some of which are included in the next chapter (see page 134).

By now you may be wondering if I ever recommend working Magic at all? Well, of course I do, it's just that I also recommend thinking about it very carefully and working out in your mind all the possible ramifications that your Magic will have.

I also recommend keeping a record of your Magical, and other, Craft working. If you do this you will be able to see how your Magic works and what the effects are, so that in the future you can refine and improve your technique and ability. Your record is called a **Book of Shadows**, because what it contains are but the shadows of the real thing. Obviously, if you share your home with others, especially those who are not in tune with the Craft, you will have to be very careful about what you write in this book and how you can keep it away from prying eyes.

'To Know, to Will, to Dare, to Keep Silent'

There is a saying, occasionally called the Magician's rules, which really sums up the things you need for successful Magic: 'To know, to will, to dare, to keep silent.'

To *know* means to work out exactly what you want to do, precisely what change you are seeking to make, and to consider all the possible effects this may have, so that you don't create any unwelcome changes.

To *will* means that you must apply the whole force of your will, through the balance of the elements and the power of the Goddess and the God. Using the elements means bringing together your thoughts, passions, emotions and physical energy to focus on the problem and its solution, to the exclusion of all other thoughts. Then, using visualization, you direct that force, with all your energy, towards your chosen solution. This is what will make the Magic happen.

To *dare* means you must actually get on and do it. It's no use just thinking about the changes you want to make unless you are prepared to get on with making them. To dare also means believing that you can work your Magic, as even the slightest doubt in the back of your mind will weaken your will and therefore dilute your Magic.

To *keep silent* about your interest in the Craft is very important – you have to be very careful whom you tell about it and what you tell – but in a Magical context it is even more important. The first reason is because Magical energy can be diluted by others, especially if they don't fully approve of what you are doing.

The second reason is because by discussing your Magical working you dilute your own energy. Think about the last time you were really angry or upset and talked about it with a friend. Doing so would have helped to soothe your feelings and calm you down – it diluted the strength of your energy. The same applies with Magic, as you need the whole force of your convictions behind what you are trying to achieve.

There is a third reason to keep silent and that is to protect your own privacy. If you tell just one person that you are a Witch and working Magic, then chances are that word will get out. I once heard it put this way: 'How can you trust your friend to keep a secret, if you can't?'

The exception to keeping silent is when you are working with others, as everyone concerned needs to be working towards the same ends.

CHAPTER SEVEN

MAGICAL TOOLS AND THE SACRED SPACE

'Wand and pentacle and sword ...'

As I discussed earlier, before you can do any Magical work – ritual, healing, spellcasting – you need first to create a Sacred Space. Witches do not have special buildings in which they worship; they create their own space wherever and whenever they need it.

In this chapter we'll look at the tools of the Craft. In the early days of your Magical working it is helpful to have some visual keys, but once you master the Magic you'll be to do away with tools and work with the energy in its pure form. We'll also cover a step-by-step method for creating your own Sacred Space using tools.

THE TOOLS OF THE CRAFT AND SUBSTITUTIONS

The following are tools of the Craft which you will find more often used by a Coven, but alongside each I have included an alternative which is more likely to be used by the Solitary Witch. Of course it is up to you whether

you want to spend a lot of money on special equipment, but I can assure you that your Magic will be no less effective if you use a simpler alternative.

Altar: This can be a special table or more simply the surface which you clear for your working equipment.

Altar cloth: This can be as elaborate as you wish or can be a simple cloth. Of course you do not have to have one at all. Alternatively, you can use a cloth as your Altar rather than use a piece of furniture.

Pentacles: Whilst for Witches the pentacle (five-pointed star within a circle) means the balance of the elements of Earth, Air, Fire, Water and Spirit, many people have a very negative image of this symbol. There are two main kinds of pentacle: that which you place on your Altar and that worn as jewellery:

Altar pentacle: This represents both the Craft and the element of Earth. You can have a special one set aside for the Altar, perhaps made of wood or stone. You can create your own by taking a small flat stone and painting the pentacle on one side. You can use a piece of jewellery. You can draw one with salt – although this needs a little practice to get right, it is also 'disposable' and therefore vanishes when you clear away.

The use of an Altar pentacle is twofold: first to represent Earth, in which case you can use some salt or a plain stone, and secondly some Witches use it as a combined centrepiece and/or work area. You do not actually

need a pentacle as such to fulfil either of these roles – the element of Earth is a part of you and your working space can be just that, a space. You certainly shouldn't need an overt centrepiece to remind you that you're working Witchcraft!

The pentacle as jewellery: Pentacles are worn by some Witches and by some non-Witches as well. You certainly do not have to wear a pentacle to be a Witch. If you wish to wear one but do not want to be conspicuous, then look carefully at the various Celtic jewellery designs available on the market. The five-pointed star appears within many as a part of the design.

Symbol of Earth: Although the pentacle represents Earth it is usual to find salt on the Altar as well. However, if you have drawn your pentacle of salt you do not need any more. If you still wish to have a symbol of Earth then a small rock, pebble or crystal is in keeping with the nature of the element and the Craft.

Symbol of Air: In a Coven you will often find loose grain incense, charcoal and a special burner (called a censer or thurible) used to symbolize Air. You can substitute an incense stick, an oil burner (with oil), a flower or even a feather.

Symbol of Fire: The usual symbol is a candle. A tea light or nite-light is a perfectly acceptable and far less expensive form of this.

Symbol of Water: A bowl of water is the obvious symbol of this element. However, you can use a seashell, with or without water in it.

Symbols of the Goddess and the God: Many Covens will have two Altar candles, one to represent each part of the divine. Some groups will also have a statue or painting of the Goddess and of the God. The alternatives you can use for the Goddess include a stone with a hole

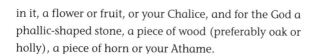

in it, a flower or fruit, or your Chalice, and for the God a phallic-shaped stone, a piece of wood (preferably oak or holly), a piece of horn or your Athame.

The Chalice: A Coven, or the High Priestess, will keep a special drinking vessel as the Chalice. This can be ornate or simple. It can be made of stone, wood, metal or glass. For a solitary Witch it is common to use an ordinary drinking glass and if possible to set this aside for ritual use only.

Athame or Wand: Many sources state that as a Witch you must have an Athame and that it should be a black-handled knife with a blade nine inches long. This is not so. Anything that you cannot accomplish with your finger, you will not be able to achieve with an Athame.

Many Witches will use a 'knife' made of wood, bone or even stone, sometimes as short as 10 centimetres – these are most commonly found as paper knives.

As an alternative you can use a wand – a piece of

straight(ish) wood around about the length of your fore-arm (from fingertips to elbow), or a little shorter, which you have gathered yourself from fallen wood. Some types of tree are thought to be more Magical than others; oak, ash, rowan, willow, for example.

A wand does not have to be decorated in any way, but you can decorate it if you wish. You can purchase fine decorated Wands from shops or by mail order. They may have crystals embedded in them, symbols carved into them and even feathers or bells tied to them, but this will not make them any more effective. It is the wood that you have gathered yourself, together with any work that you have done to it, that will have the most personal power.

OTHER SUBSTITUTIONS IN RITUAL

Many of you reading this book may live with others who are not interested or even in favour of the Craft, so I have included here a few suggestions for changes you may

need to make so that your ritual does not offend those you live with:

Candles: Burning candles may well cause concern; many people are quite rightly worried about the safety of this practice. A good substitute is to use a quartz crystal, which reflects the light of Fire, or a gemstone with a Fire correspondence, such as sunstone or tiger's eye.

Incense: Using incense can often cause offence. Rather than burning incense you can use an oil burner, or anoint objects with essential or perfumed oils. Alternatively, you can use flowers of the appropriate season. You don't have to spend a lot of money on them, just one or two blooms will be enough.

Speaking: Whilst in a group environment it is important for you to speak (or chant or sing) clearly and audibly. When alone it is not the volume that you use which is

important, it is the intent with which you work your rituals and Magic. The Goddess and the God do not require you to speak aloud – any words can be said in your head.

Wine: Some Witches do not drink alcohol anyway, so you are not alone in seeking a substitute for this. Non-alcoholic wine is an option but far better is fruit juice, preferably something indigenous to your country, so for example apple would be a good choice in Britain.

Cakes: The cakes of 'Wine and Cakes' are in fact a form of biscuit made from three ingredients and cut into the shape of the Crescent Moon. When working on your own it is quite all right to use any kind of commercially available biscuit or even a piece of fruit.

Other tools: There are many other things which can be added to the above list, but they are not essential. As mentioned earlier, when working in a group the use of

visual keys is useful, but when working on your own you do not necessarily need these things.

CREATING YOUR SACRED SPACE

To use your tools, you will have to find a time and place when you are certain of being undisturbed. The first step is then to 'centre yourself'. By this I mean to relax your mind to clear it of everyday distractions whilst also focusing it on what you are about to do. Many people find that it is helpful to wash and put on a special item of clothing, then to gather together all the things you are going to need. It can also be useful to do a few breathing exercises; just breathing in and out slowly and rhythmically whilst concentrating only on your breathing can do wonders for your ability to focus.

Lay your tools out upon your cloth. Where you place them is not fixed, although it is usual to place the symbols of the elements around the outside in accordance with their corresponding points of the compass, and it is wise to place any candles, if you are using them, at the back, so you do not have to reach over them. Leave a space in the centre for any special items you need for your actual working.

Having brought symbols of the elements, it is necessary to bless and consecrate them, which is done by either placing your Athame into or onto that item or by holding your hands over each (to the sides if you are using anything hot) and saying, *'I do bless and consecrate this symbol of [Earth, Air, Fire, Water] to make it fit for my rites. Blessed Be.'* (If you are using salt to symbolize Earth, remember it does not need to be consecrated, as salt is deemed to be pure already.)

Next you need to summon the elements themselves. In a Coven, this is usually performed by different members of the group in turn moving to and facing each elemental direction and drawing the appropriate invoking pentagram, whilst all perform the necessary

visualizations. However, when you are working on your own it is not necessary to perform the 'actions'.

We start with the element of Air, as it represents our thoughts and should therefore come first. Visualize the air itself – clouds racing across the sky, treetops blowing. See it in your mind's eye coming from the east. Remember that Air is our thoughts, it is spring and new beginnings. When you are confident that you have Air with you, say, *'I call upon the element of Air to be with me, to watch over me, to guard, guide and protect me during these my rites. Blessed Be.'* At first you may find it helpful to do this with your eyes closed, but later you will find that you can visualize over what you see in the 'real' world. After you have done this for Air, repeat it for Fire (which comes from the south), then Water (from the west) and finally Earth (from the north).

Now you need to invite the presence of the Goddess and the God. Here you visualize the Goddess and the God, in whichever forms appeal to you or are appropriate for your working. I find it helpful to imagine them coming as if from a distance and getting closer. See them as smiling and welcoming. When you are sure that you can see them well, say, *'I call upon the Lord and Lady to watch over me, to guard, guide and protect me during these my rites. Blessed Be.'*

The last step in creating your Sacred Space is to cast the Circle. The Circle should encompass the whole of the working space and its boundary should not be crossed during the course of your ritual. This is one of the reasons for careful preparation prior to your ritual. You should not need to leave the Circle to go and fetch anything you have forgotten. If you do have to leave the Circle, you will have to open a doorway in the Circle, close it behind you and then get whatever you need. On your return you will again have to open a doorway and close it behind you. But to return to casting your Circle, in a Coven this will be done by one member walking the outside boundary of the Circle and, using an Athame, or the Coven sword,

drawing a ring of protection whilst visualizing an electric blue light. This ring then 'flows' to become a sphere which encompasses the whole area, not just on the horizontal plane, but also above and below.

When working on your own, you can remain in the centre and visualize drawing the Circle using either your Athame or your finger. Start at the north-east point and draw the Circle in a clockwise direction, visualizing an electric blue light which spreads to form a sphere. As you do so, say, *'I conjure this Circle as a place between the worlds, a time out of time, a place of containment and protection. Blessed Be.'* Make sure that the line overlaps at the beginning/end point.

Clockwise is also known as Sunwise, or in the Craft as Deosil, and everything which moves within the Circle should move in this direction. Hence when the elements are called you imagine Air joining you from the east, Fire from the south, and so on.

Now your Sacred Space is complete and this is when

you perform whatever working you have created it for, whether Magic or the celebration of a Sabbat.

Towards the end of your ritual, you may wish to perform the **Rite of Wine and Cakes**, which is the blessing and consecration of wine and cakes to share the blessing of the Goddess and the God, or the Great Rite, which celebrates the union of the Goddess and the God for the fruitfulness of the land and people. As the two rites are quite similar, although performed for different purposes, here I have combined them, so that in your ritual you can use your intent to direct your rite towards whichever purpose seems more appropriate.

For this you will need a Chalice of wine and an Athame (or the ritual substitutions) and a plate with a cake or biscuit.

Take your Chalice and hold it in both hands in front of you at eye level. Focus on your visualization of the

Goddess and say, *'Behold the Chalice, symbol of the Goddess, the Great Mother who brings fruitfulness and knowledge to all.'*

Place the Chalice down and take your Athame. Hold this in both hands in front of you, blade pointing upwards, also at eye level, and, focusing on the image of the God, say, *'Behold the Athame, symbol of the God, the All Father who brings energy and strength to all.'*

Then change the position of your Athame so that you are holding it blade downwards in your right, or strong, hand. Take the Chalice in the other hand and, lowering the blade into the wine, say, *'Joined in union together, they bring life to all.'*

Kiss the handle of your Athame and say, *'Blessed Be,'* then put it down.

Take a sip of the wine, reflecting upon the bounty of the Goddess and the strength of the God, and focus this feeling on the purpose that your ritual was conducted for.

Next take the cake (or biscuit) in your left (or weak)

hand and take your Athame in your right (or strong) hand. Place the tip of the Athame on to the cake and say, *'With this symbol of the God, I consecrate this symbol of the bounty of the Great Mother. Let their love sustain my spirit as food sustains my body. Blessed Be.'*

Replace your Athame on the Altar and take a bite of the cake.

Any remaining wine can be drunk, and cake eaten, as part of your feasting, or if you prefer, you may take it outside later and pour it or put it on the ground as a libation to nature.

Having completed the focus of your ritual and celebrated with the Goddess and the God, all that remains is to tidy away after yourself. This has to be done in two stages, first on the spiritual plane by removing the Sacred Space and then on the physical plane by putting away all your tools and returning the area to its normal

purpose and appearance.

The first thing to do is to remove the Circle. Starting again at the north-east point, redraw the same line, but this time visualize the sphere and Circle melting and disappearing. Say, *'I remove this Circle and return this place and this time to their own. Blessed Be.'*

Next you thank the Goddess and the God, visualizing them in the same way as before. Say, *'I give thanks to the Lord and Lady for being with me, for guarding, guiding and protecting me, and I bid them Hale and Farewell. Blessed Be.'* Now visualize them going away from you, perhaps receding into the distance in the opposite direction to that in which they appeared.

Then it is time to banish the elements. Again starting in the east, visualize Air with all its attributes, say, *'I give thanks to the element of Air for watching over me, guarding, guiding and protecting me. Blessed Be,'* and then visualize it fading from view. Repeat this with each of the elements in turn.

Try to make sure that you do this carefully and completely, as you do not want to leave residual elemental influences in your environment. The results are not so much dangerous as inconvenient. I know of people who have failed to banish Water and have had a burst pipe, or who have failed to banish Fire and had electrical equipment fail to work. If you are at any time interrupted in your work, do remember to go back later to banish whatever you summoned earlier, so as to leave the spiritual plane clear for your use in the future.

Lastly, return the physical space to its normal purpose and appearance. Please remember to extinguish any candles or incense extremely carefully and never leave a burning candle unattended, not even for a moment. At this point you should make sure that you eat and drink something in order to fully ground yourself.

CHAPTER EIGHT

SPELLS, CHARMS AND POTIONS

'Let the Magic come to life …'

Now you're ready to start casting your spells!

You will find after you have read, or tried, a few of the spells in this chapter that there are several themes which start to recur. Once you can see this pattern you will find it easy to devise spells of your own choosing. Here I will give you some visual keys to work with, although as you become more experienced you may find that you do not always need to use them. As I have already mentioned, probably the most important thing about getting your Magic right is to ensure that you fully understand the problem and that you are confident that your solution will not cause any other problems, so don't forget this preparatory ground.

In each of the following spells, I have assumed that you will be working within the Circle, even though in some cases you will need to take something, perhaps an empowered stone or herb preparation, out of it for use.

The Magical Power of Herbs

The use of herbs and plants is an integral part of the Craft and is a practice which goes back many centuries. Herbal work is simply an extension of Spellcraft which uses the natural energies of the plants around us to complement and sustain our Magic. In this chapter I have included a variety of Magical recipes involving the use of herbs or plants – either in essential oil form or in herb form.

Here is a brief description of some of the more easily available and useful herbs and plants:

Basil: Protection, study, concentration, memory, examinations, strength

Bergamot: To relieve depression, negativity, regret

Black pepper: Opening, stimulating, penetrating

Camomile: Rest, peace, soothing

Cardamom: Clarity, passion

Cedar: Stress relief, focus

Cinnamon: The Sun, psychic awareness

Clary Sage: Balance, psychic ability

Clove: The Goddess as Crone, divination, prosperity

Eucalpytus: Colds and flu

Fennel: Travel, dietary control

Frankincense: The God, the Sun, purifying, protection, preparation for ritual, emotional healing, courage, insecurity

Ginger: Self-acceptance, courage, strength

Jasmine: The Goddess, the Moon, divination, dreams, love, self-acceptance

Lavender: Healing of all kinds, rest and sleep, travel

Melissa: The Goddess as Mother, woman, female aspect

Myrrh: The Goddess as Crone, wisdom, knowledge, banishing negativity

Neroli (which is orange blossom and not to be confused with niaouli): Stress relief, romance, exhaustion

Patchouli: Clarity, passion

Peppermint: Strength, studying, mental stimulation

Pine: Mental cleansing

Rose: The Goddess as Mother, psychic awareness,

romance, emotional healing, grief

Rosemary: Clarity, study, memory, indecisiveness

Sage: Prosperity, tonic, stimulating

Sandalwood: The God, the Moon, courage, self-confidence, perseverance

Tea tree: Antiseptic, healing infections

Thyme: Psychic awareness, travel, relief of colds and flu

Ylang ylang: The Goddess as Maiden, romance, self-appreciation, mental stability

If using essential oils, make sure that they really are 100 per cent essential oils, not perfumed blends or blended oils. There are many cheap, and not so cheap, fakes on the market, so it is worth taking the extra time and effort to track down the real thing and pay the proper price for it.

Do not use essential oils, other than lavender, on pregnant women, nursing mothers, babies or children under 12 without consulting an experienced aromatherapist.

SPELLS FOR LOVE AND RELATIONSHIPS

TO ATTRACT NEW FRIENDS OR A PARTNER

As I mentioned earlier, it is not a good idea to seek to tie an individual to yourself or to another, however it is perfectly acceptable to ask the Goddess and the God to bring a suitable companion, or companions, your way. In this you are not interfering with the will of others, but are seeking the opportunity to meet those with whom you stand a chance of developing a good relationship.

This is one of those spells where you need to be careful what you ask for. It is no good saying you want someone handsome – they may turn out to be a rat! Try to focus on personality rather than appearance and be very wary of making a 'closed' request. If you find yourself thinking of a particular individual, then please, stop doing the spell. By far the best way to phrase your request is to focus on 'someone I will be happy with and

who will be happy with me'. This spell is best done during the New or Waxing Moon.

This spell is one where you need nothing other than your ability to visualize and concentrate. Once you have created your Sacred Space, again visualize the Goddess and the God watching over you. Speak to them in the same way that you would to anyone you greatly respect and love. Ask them, in your heart, for the opportunity to meet and get to know the right person (if you are seeking a partner) or people (if seeking more friends). Take your time doing this and when you are sure they have heard you, thank them in advance. Remove your Circle as before.

It is customary, when working with Magic directly for your own benefit, to also make a 'payment' for this, preferably in advance. So sometime soon after you have worked this Circle, find the time to do something for the Goddess and the God. This can be as simple as planting a herb or flower, or even dedicating a disliked task to them, but do make sure that you really do mean it.

Don't expect your Magic to take instant effect. It is extremely unlikely that the very next person to come along will be brought into your life as a result of your Magic. Think of it this way – it takes time to weave the threads of Fate so that the right person can be brought your way.

This spell is sometimes used by those who are seeking a Coven or a teacher in the Craft.

To Reconcile Differences

These can be differences between yourself and another or between two other people. If you decide to work Magic you have to bear in mind that there is only a limited amount you can do before you step over the line of interfering in other people's lives. But that is not to say that you should do nothing. Sometimes all that is needed is for both parties to be given the opportunity to speak and to listen with understanding. Obviously, the earlier you can

do this in a quarrel, the more likely you are to have positive results. The best time to perform this spell is during the week before the Full Moon to three days after.

This is a spell which needs to take place over several days and whilst it is started in the Circle, the subsequent steps do not need to be performed in one.

You will need either a picture of each person (even a very rough sketch that you have drawn yourself will suffice) or an object to represent each and three small pieces of wood (used matches work very well).

In your Circle you need to formally name both pictures or objects. Here I have named the parties Adam and Beryl, but you will give them the names by which they are known to you (which might be a shortened form of their real names or even a nickname).

Take the first picture and, holding it up to the Goddess and the God, say, *'I name this "Adam", by Air and Fire, Water and Earth, and before the Lord and Lady,*

this is Adam. Blessed Be.' Whilst you say this you will need to visualize each of the elements, the Goddess and the God, as you mention them, so take your time.

Put that picture down, take up the picture of Beryl and repeat the process.

Take the three pieces of wood, hold them up and say, *'These three are the obstacles to Adam and Beryl resolving their differences. As each is removed, so their opportunity to meet, talk and listen in truth, honesty and respect are increased, and if the Lord and Lady will it, so their chances of reconciliation draw closer.'*

Place each picture, separated by the three 'obstacles', somewhere where you will be able to leave them undisturbed for three days and nights. This completes the part you will work in the Circle.

On each of the three successive days, at the same time, you will need to remove one of the pieces of wood and draw the two pictures that bit closer, so that when all the 'obstacles' have gone the pictures are touching.

As you remove each piece of wood, visualize the two coming closer together. Dispose of the wood by taking it outside and driving it into the ground. Leave the pictures together for a further three nights if you can.

Remember, though, that it may not be intended that these two ever do resume their relationship in the way you hope for. However, you have done your best to ensure that they at least have the chance to communicate and perhaps to be reconciled. Remember not to talk to them, or to anyone else, about this spell, for the reasons set out earlier.

The method of formally naming a picture, or a symbol, can be used for other purposes. Suppose you are trying to find a work opportunity for someone for whom you cannot prepare a talisman for one reason or another (I'll talk more about talismans later in the chapter) – perhaps a third party whose aid has been sought by a friend. You can give an item their identity in order to work this Magic on their behalf. Give another

symbolic item, perhaps a 'coin', the 'identity' of a job offer and bring the two together in the same way.

OTHER WITCHY TIPS

⚹ Herb sachets are excellent ways of working magic for yourself or for others. In addition to herbs, flowers, spices, leaves, and so on, they may also contain stones, charms or crystals, all imbued with magical energies.

The sachets can be made from almost any natural fabric; it does not have to be specially bought for the purpose. Make sure the fabric is thoroughly washed and if you have any doubts about its psychic cleanliness then hang it overnight in the light of the Full Moon before use. The easiest shape to use is a circle, but a square also looks quite attractive. Place your ingredients in the centre and tie up all the ends to create a bundle. To tie your sachet(s) you can use thread, cord, ribbon or even twine or string.

Remember whilst making up your sachet to keep your Magical goals clearly in mind and to imbue it with Magical power.

To find your true love, carry this sachet with you at all times.

2 parts rose petals

2 parts jasmine flowers

1 part lavender

1 part sandalwood

If you can, add a small rose quartz crystal to the mix and place the whole in pink cloth tied with silver cord.

A word of caution, though: do not assume that the first person you meet after preparing this is the right one!

Aromatherapy oils not only smell nice but also contain airborne components which can actually alter the mood of not only the wearer but also of those around them.

✻ **When preparing for a romantic encounter**, whether out on a date or at home with a loved one, have a long relaxing soak in the bath in the following:

2 drops sandalwood oil

2 drops jasmine oil

1 drop neroli oil

1 drop ylang ylang oil

Blend the oils with a teaspoonful of unscented base oil or a tablespoonful of unscented bath foam before adding to the bath – my personal favourite is the plain foaming bath oil from The Body Shop.

If you really want to add spice to the encounter, add 1 drop of cardamom oil, but be prepared for the results!

✻ **To appear more attractive to others**, try the following blend of essential oils. It can be used in the bath for a subtle effect or blended with a base oil to make a perfume. When using the blend in this way it should always be applied sparingly.

3 drops jasmine oil

3 drops neroli oil

3 drops ylang ylang oil

<ul>
<li>

To calm a tense atmosphere, try a blend of the following essential oils. Again they can be used in the bath or blended with a base oil to make a perfume. Alternatively, use this recipe in an oil burner, especially at tense or disruptive times.

5 drops frankincense oil

3 drops jasmine oil

</li>

<li>

To improve communication in any relationship, bathe with the following or use in an oil burner.

4 drops rosemary oil

2 drops sandalwood oil

2 drops jasmine oil

2 drops ylang ylang oil

1 drop cedarwood oil

</li>
</ul>

SPELLS FOR CLEANSING AND PROTECTION

TO BANISH PERSONAL NEGATIVITY

From time to time we all feel influenced by negative thoughts and feelings. These may be caused by the way we feel about ourselves, the things others have said or an unpleasant experience. Banishing, or driving away, is best done during the Waning Moon or on a Saturday.

To banish these feelings you will need a small bowl of water and some salt. After you have created your Sacred Space, consecrate the water by dipping your Athame, or finger, into it and saying, *'I bless and consecrate this water to drive out all impurities and make it pure and fit for these my rites. Blessed Be.'*

Next, bless the salt, sprinkle some onto your Altar cloth and again using your finger or Athame, say, *'I bless this salt to make it fit for these my rites. Blessed Be.'*

Now add a little salt to the water and hold the bowl up

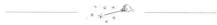

towards the Goddess and the God. Visualize them being present and say, *'I ask the Lord and Lady to let this be the receiver of all my negativity, so that I might cleanse myself and become whole once more. Blessed Be.'*

Place the bowl down safely, dip the fingers and thumbs of both hands into the water and visualize all negative thoughts and feelings moving through your body, down through your arms and out from your hands into the water. As you do this, be aware of yourself becoming lighter, of losing the weight that has been on your mind.

When you are sure that all is completed, remove your hands, shaking the last drops of water from them into the bowl. Take a moment to centre yourself once more and again holding the bowl up to the Goddess and the God, say, *'I ask the Lord and Lady to take this negativity and through their power and the power of the elements to keep me safe in their hands. Blessed Be.'*

This rite is often used in conjunction with others as it enables you to cleanse your mind fully before moving on

to other work. If this is the only rite you intend to perform you can now remove your Sacred Space. When all is done pour the 'contaminated' water away onto the earth (not near anything you are trying to grow) or down the drain.

To Banish Negativity from a Room or to Cleanse and Protect an Area

You may sometimes feel that a room or your home has been affected by negative influences. Perhaps you have had someone unpleasant there or there has been an argument. In this case you can use a similar method.

The following spell should be performed as soon as you feel the need and then reinforced during the next Waning Moon.

Again in your Circle, consecrate and bless the salt and water as above. Add the salt to the water and, holding it up to the Goddess and the God, say, *'I ask the Lord and Lady to let this water drive out all negative influences. Blessed Be.'* Put the bowl safely to one side.

Next take a sprig of rosemary, or a small amount of the dried herb tied in a small cloth, and, holding it up to the Goddess and the God, say, *'I ask the Lord and Lady to empower this herb that it might guard my place from all negative thoughts and persons. Blessed Be.'*

Visualize the Goddess and the God directing their energy towards and into the herb, so that it becomes charged with their power. Then hold it between your hands and visualize each of the elements in turn adding their power to it – the earth that it was grown in, the air that stirred its leaves, the Sunlight and the rain which enabled it to grow. When you feel that the herb is empowered, put it to one side.

Now you can remove your Sacred Space. Take your bowl of water and gently sprinkle it around the outside edge of the area you wish to cleanse, moving clockwise or Deosil. You do not need a continuous flow of drops or to soak everything in order to perform this. As you go, visualize the drops joining up to make a barrier which drives

negativity out and through which it cannot return.

Finally, take your empowered rosemary and pin it up over the entrance to the area you wish to protect.

OTHER WITCHY TIPS

✳ **If you feel concerned about negative influences or thoughts coming your way,** hang a small herb sachet of this in each window (you can hide them behind the curtains if you wish) and above each external door.

3 parts rosemary

2 parts fennel seed

1 part juniper

1 part dill seed

1 dried chilli pepper

1 part the outer dry skin of garlic

1 part coarse salt (rock salt)

Place in a red cloth tied with a black cord. If you think you know who might be harbouring negative thoughts

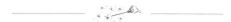

about you, then you can also place a small mirror facing outwards in the window which most closely points in their direction. This will reflect back any negativity.

* **For safety and protection for the car/motorbike,** place the following into violet cloth tied with a cord of the same (or similar) colour as your vehicle:

3 parts rosemary

2 parts juniper

2 parts basil

1 part fennel

1 part coarse salt (rock salt)

a few drops of peppermint oil

Place the sachet in the glove compartment or suspend it from the rear-view mirror.

This formula works just as well for a motorcycle – place it in one of the panniers or carry it on your person when riding.

✴ **To remove negative influences**, whether internal negativity or that felt from others, make the following herbs into a 'tea' and add them to your bath. You will need to steep the herbs in a small amount of boiling water for around 15 to 20 minutes and then strain the resultant liquid into your bath.

4 teaspoons rosemary

2 teaspoons lavender

1 teaspoon crushed juniper berries

4 crushed bay leaves

1 teaspoon salt

In addition to the herbs, some people also recommend placing a clear quartz crystal into the bath to absorb any negative influences. Make sure you remove this before pulling the plug, so as not to lose it, and then rinse it under cold running water for 10 minutes to cleanse it.

SPELLS FOR LUCK AND MONEY
TO ASSURE YOUR HOUSEHOLD'S FINANCIAL SECURITY

When working Magic for money you have to be very careful what you ask for. Simply asking for money could result in inheriting it from a loved one or receiving it from an insurance claim. It is far better to work for the opportunity to earn money. Also, money does not exist in the natural world, and the Craft is about working with natural forces, so again it would be better to work to ensure that you can meet your needs.

To cover all the normal expenses, bills, and so on, firstly cut out a circle, six inches across, from a piece of yellow/orange paper or card. On it draw a pentacle so that the points just touch the edge of the paper circle. In the centre of the pentacle write the initials of all the members of your household. Within the points of the pentacle either write, or draw, small pictures to represent the things you need money to cover, for example, house, bills, food and drink, pets, car, and so on. Try to cover all the things you need, but don't be tempted to ask for more than that as this will dilute the Magic. Take your time over creating this talisman so that you put as much personal energy into it as possible. At the next Full Moon anoint each of the points of the pentacle with a blend of jasmine and cedar oil, and ask the Goddess and the God to bless this talisman to bring sufficient income to your house to maintain your family's financial security. Hang it high, as near to the centre of the house as you can. You can also make miniatures of this talisman and give one to every earner in the household to carry in their purse or wallet.

OTHER WITCHY TIPS

🎇 **To increase good fortune and bring money your way**, hang this sachet over the main entrance to the house and bury a coin just outside the door so that everyone entering has to pass over it. This charm

does not guarantee untold wealth, but it does work to give you the opportunities to ensure that you have enough for your needs. Tie the following in a green cloth with a gold cord:

2 parts basil

2 parts mint

1 part jasmine

1 part pine kernels

1 part rice

1 whole nutmeg

1 almond

5 star anise seeds

✳ **To increase your opportunities to earn money**, use the following to anoint a special coin, and keep this coin in your purse. It does not have to be common currency – you could use a foreign or old coin. Make sure you do not spend this one!

3 drops basil oil

2 drops ginger oil

1 drop vanilla essence or extract (not flavouring)

❋ **When seeking new work**, take a green candle and anoint it with the above oils, and then burn it on three successive nights, until it is all gone. Whilst burning the candle, visualize the kind of work or employment you are looking for, starting from the moment you find the advertisement, or opening, and continuing to visualize right up to the point where you get the letter telling you your application has been successful. This is best performed at the Waxing or Full Moon, and even better if you can start on a Wednesday.

SPELLS FOR HEALING

I discussed the pros and cons of healing earlier. To recap briefly, you need to be sure that by performing healing you are not aggravating a problem or prolonging suffering. When you have carefully considered how best a problem may be solved, however, then you are in a position to do something to help it.

Healing Magic is best performed as soon as the problem comes to light. The Full Moon is considered a more effective time, but, unless the timing is right, I should use that as a time to reinforce your spell rather than waiting.

TO ASK FOR HELP WITH HEALING

The simplest form of request is to ask the Goddess and the God to watch over and help the person (or animal) you are working for. Once again, this, like many of the spells I have given you, leaves the decision-making up to the Goddess and the God, who are, after all, probably best placed to make it.

Take into your Circle with you something which represents the person you are working for. It could be a picture or it could just be something which you feel symbolizes them. Name it in the same way as in the spell on reconciling differences (see page 126) and, holding it up to the Goddess and the God, simply ask for healing for them.

If, however, you have a good idea of what is wrong and of the way in which nature would put it right, you can direct your spell in quite a different way. Visualize the person before the Goddess and the God and visualize the natural healing process taking place, driven and enhanced by their power, until you can clearly see the person whole and well again.

I cannot stress enough, though, that anyone who seeks physical healing through the Craft should always seek conventional treatments too. It gives confirmation of diagnosis, and conventional and Craft healing are very compatible.

In cases where the problem is emotional or spiritual, perhaps when a person is overcome with grief, then the healing process you are visualizing relates to the process of coming to terms with their loss and achieving personal balance.

EARTH OR NATURE HEALING

Almost every Witch has a pet cause or environmental problem they feel particularly concerned about. This could be cruelty to animals, the plight of the dolphin or an endangered species or simply the overall damage to our planet.

Whilst it is not really within the power of any one Witch to cure such global problems, the work that each of us performs does make a difference. Our Magical work contributes towards reversing the trends and bringing back nature's balance. Where we direct our energy towards assisting an organization already committed to solving the problem, perhaps by working towards making their views heard, we can often find that a little Magic goes a long way. This kind of general environmental healing is best performed at the Full Moon and the Sabbats, especially Beltane.

One of the most potent ways of providing Magical assistance is often called 'Raising the Dragon'. In your Circle, visualize a great dragon curled up inside the planet. Take your time envisaging its appearance and, if you can, colour it in sympathy with your chosen cause.

Call to it with your heart and mind and empower it with your energy, wake it and when you feel that you have its attention, tell it of the problem and of the results you would like to see. Tell it also that you are asking it to contribute its own energies and that once it has worked its own Magic that it may return, with your thanks, to its home.

Then, with all your strength, get it to rise out of its lair and flying clockwise, or Deosil, to go to the problem. Once you have released the dragon, watch it with your

mind's eye and you will see it fly around the globe three times. Once it begins its descent to the land you may release the image, as your part is done.

Remember to be careful what you wish for and choose a specific problem – do not simply work for 'the good of the planet'. After all, one way of healing Mother Earth might be to remove all the people!

Do not perform this ritual more than once a month, as it can, and should, require a lot of personal energy and to do it too often will almost certainly result in you becoming drained.

Other Witchy Tips

✳ **To help a person who is unwell**, wrap the following ingredients in a violet cloth tied with violet ribbon and anoint the sachet on each side with 3 drops of eucalyptus oil.

2 parts lavender

2 parts cinnamon

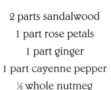

2 parts sandalwood
1 part rose petals
1 part ginger
1 part cayenne pepper
½ whole nutmeg

Carry the sachet on your person or hang it over the bed of anyone who is unwell. As soon as the illness is over the sachet should be destroyed.

The first thing to do when destroying sachets is to remember to give thanks to the Goddess and the God. It is not enough to just accept the Magic, you need to try to give back something too. Perhaps plant a useful herb in your garden or, alternatively, spend some time working on the land or clearing rubbish from your local park.

After you have given something back, then it is time to dispose of the sachet. Open it and scatter all the environmentally-friendly parts to the winds. Stones, crystals and charms should be buried or cast into the sea or a stream. The fabric of the sachet and any paper, perhaps

with your intent written on, can be burned or torn into shreds and buried.

 **To promote healing or before performing any healing Magic**, drink the following herbal tea. To make the tea, pour half a pint of boiling water over the herbs listed below. Allow the fusion to stand for 10 minutes before straining and do not stir, as this bruises the plants. If you prefer your tea sweet, add a little honey, not sugar, to the strained infusion.

1 teaspoon rosemary

1 teaspoon rosehips

(or a couple of teaspoons of rosehip syrup)

½ teaspoon sage

1 teaspoon thyme

Do not drink this tea more than three times a day – you can have too much of a good thing!

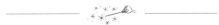

⚹ **As soon as you feel the onset of a cold or flu**, have a long relaxing soak in the following:

4 drops lavender oil

2 drops eucalpytus oil

2 drops jasmine oil

1 drop cinnamon oil

1 drop ginger oil

Blend the oils with a tablespoonful of unscented bath foam or a teaspoonful of unscented oil before adding to the bath.

After bathing, wrap up warmly and go to bed with a warm drink.

⚹ We all have times in our lives when we need to care for our own physical, mental and emotional state. In fact most of us neglect ourselves in these respects far too often. But if you do not look after yourself, how are you going to do the best for those you care for? Take time out at least once a week to treat your-

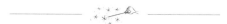

self. Make the environment as pleasant as you can –
perhaps light candles around the bath and play
some soothing music. Above all, turn off the phone
and lock the door to make sure you are not disturbed even by your near and dear. Then relax in
the following **self-care bath** (as before, blend oils
with a teaspoonful of base oil or a tablespoonful of
base bath foam):

2 drops frankincense oil

2 drops jasmine oil

2 drops sandalwood oil

2 drops ylang ylang oil

1 drop rose oil

1 drop ginger oil

CREATING A TALISMAN

A talisman is simply a portable object which has been
empowered for a purpose. You can easily create a

talisman for almost any purpose, say self-confidence, interview courage, creativity, concentration, exam success or protection, using the method below.

First you have to select an appropriate object. It needs to be something which can easily be carried. For this reason a piece of jewellery is often chosen. However, you may not have the money for jewellery, or the inclination to wear it, so you can always select a small stone which can be kept in the pocket or purse. If you purchase something, you will need to prepare the object by cleansing it of all outside influences. You can either place it under running water for five minutes, while visualizing all imperfections being washed away, as already mentioned, or you can place it overnight in the light of the Full Moon, in which case it will be additionally empowered by this process. If you prefer to use something you have found, such as a pebble or even a small piece of wood, it is a good idea to wash it to remove any excess dirt, but you do not need to cleanse it in the same way if

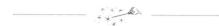

you are sure that it has been in the elements and not handled by anyone else.

In your Circle, take your talisman and bless and consecrate it by the same process used for the rosemary in the spell on page 136, but this time ask the Lord and Lady that it perform whichever function you have chosen. When you are confident that it is ready, put it to one side if it is for your personal use until the time comes when you need it. When that time comes wear or carry your talisman from the moment you set out to the moment your desire is fulfilled. If you have prepared it for someone else, wrap it in a small cloth or paper until you are ready to give it to them. This stops it getting handled before it gets to its new owner.

There are many books of spells available and some are filled with detailed lists of what you will need to make your Magic work. However, the Magic comes from within you, from your knowledge of the elements, the Goddess and the God. It works through your ability to concentrate and focus, and to visualize. These are the techniques you need to practise. The other things which will enhance your Magic are the use of the appropriate times of the Moon and, particularly when working for yourself, the use of herbs and other plants.

A FINAL WORD

This has been a brief look at the Craft today – I hope that you've enjoyed it and found it useful. Remember that the more you practise your Craft, and get in touch with the Goddess and the God both within and outside of you, the more reliable your results will be. Good luck and happy Spellcasting.

Blessed Be.